TRUCK RACING

MIKE KEY

*Circuit, drag, oval & desert truck racing
from America, Africa & Europe*

Published in 1988 by Osprey Publishing Limited
27A Floral Street, London WC2E 9DP
Member company of the George Philip Group

British Library Cataloguing in Publication Data.
Key, Mike
  Truck racing.
  1. Lorries. Racing
  I. Title
  796.7′2
ISBN 0-85045-811-0

Editor Tony Thacker
Design Simon Bell

Printed in Hong Kong

Page 1

Mack truck in full flight. Raphy Gorret, from
Switzerland, races head-on in his 14 litre,
turbocharged 1974 Mack with overdrive
gearbox. Raphy became interested in truck
racing through an article in a Swiss magazine,
Camions

About the author

**Mike Key began his career at the dragstrip,
photographing the kind of vehicles he likes
best—big-engined American cars. His
dedication soon resulted in his photographs
appearing in a plethora of automotive
magazines all over the world. His interest in
drag racing soon led him to discover street
rods, customs and big American trucks.**

**   *Truck Racing* is his fifth assignment for
Osprey, his previous titles, *Tri-Chevy*, *Lead
Sleds*, *1932 Ford Street Rods* and *Fins & The
Fifties* (which he shared with Tony Thacker)
being full-colour pictorial essays on various
aspects of American auto culture.**

**   Mike lives in Norwich, England, with his
wife and two children, and several garages
full of early American automobilia.**

This book is dedicated to truckers everywhere

Pages 2–3

All the way from Czechoslovakia comes Jiri
Moskal with his Liaz, which has a six-cylinder
11.94 litre engine. The team who prepared the
Liaz trucks have also competed in the gruelling
Paris–Dakar Marathon Rally for the past three
years. In fact, in 1986, Jiri was leading that rally
until he became stuck on a narrow section and
lost the lead to an Italian entry, having to be
satisfied with second place

Where did it all begin?

Like a lot of crazes, truck racing originated in the USA, the first race being held in June 1979 at the banked super-speedway in Atlanta, Georgia. In the crowd was Andrew Frankl, publisher of *TRUCK* magazine, fresh from competing in the illegal trans-American Cannonball run. Frankl had entered *TRUCK*'s project Transit in the race from Darien, Connecticut, to Redondo Beach, California, and although the British truck came last, it did at least finish.

While in America, Frankl had been told of the historic truck race to be held in Atlanta and was determined to attend. He even managed some laps in the Capri-V6 powered Transit, before the thundering Macks and Kenworths took to the track.

History tells us that the winner of that first Great American Truck Race was Mike Adams. Enthusiasm was so high after the race that a second event was arranged at the Ontario race track near Los Angeles, California. Like some of the famous Californian drag strips, this track no longer exists, but truck racing became firmly established after the event there. In 1980 a series of races was organized by Linn Hendershoot, one of the leading lights behind the Atlanta race. These events took place in Rockingham, North Carolina, Atlanta, Georgia, and Nashville, Tennessee. It seems that there were no rules applied to the first race, but a set was drawn up for this new series, making the racing safer and faster. Pole position at every one of those events was taken by 'Charging' Charlie

Baker from Pennsylvania, one of the sport's most successful racers. In 1986 he took the Championship.

I remember my own introduction to the sport, watching a *World of Sport* **TV** programme. There it was, the much talked about truck racing from the good old USA. One particular incident is still fresh in my memory today; Ken Farmer's super red truck blew a front tyre and suffered a horrendous crash. The truck was pulled apart and the bonnet ripped off to expose the chrome engine. It tore me apart to see such a beautiful machine go to its death at 120 mph. Later, some of the crash footage was used in the film *Smokey and the Bandit*.

Another spectator at the first American truck race was Dutchman Bertus van Holland. Although, in Britain, we were slow to find suitable tracks to race on, Bertus returned from the States filled with enthusiasm and soon organized the first truck race outside the USA at his local track at Zandvoort. Obviously, the event looked different, for in place of the Peterbilts, Kenworths and Internationals, there were Scanias and DAFs.

In those early days, Bertus even found time to drive in the races himself, while still earning a living from driving a truck. Today, however, as president of the European Truck Race Organization, he is too busy running events at Zolder, Zandvoort and Hockenheim, and acting as an adviser at other truck races, such as that held at Nurburgring.

Above
Bright-red Detroit Diesel V8 engine, with plenty of plumbing for cooling and for the turbo plus supercharger

Left
From Finland comes Reima Soderman with his Sisu SR 500, which is powered by a Cummins engine. Reima is a member of the Finnish truck racing team

Where were the British during the early days of European truck racing? In September 1983 Mel Bacon shared a drive in a T45 Roadtrain, backed by Leyland France, with French racing driver Jean Louis Schlesser. The venue was the famous Le Mans circuit, and the event was the *24 Heures du Camion*, a mixture of out and out racing, economy driving and various other truck-related events, including tyre

changing, which is no mean feat on a truck. Emblazoned with a Union Jack, that particular truck is still racing today under the famous name *Gertie*.

Truck racing was an immediate success with the French, 100,000 of whom were attracted to Le Mans. The event still takes place today, every other year.

'Truck racing is great,' exclaimed Andrew Frankl to anyone in Great Britain who would listen. *TRUCK* magazine published articles on the up and coming sport in America, and on the Le Mans event, but it would be five years before a similar event took place on British soil.

Martin Hayes, at the time PR director for Leyland Vehicles, and Peter Chambers, of Leyland's Multipart Marketing Department, were two people who did listen to Frankl. Former racer, Chambers, thought it would be a fantastic way to promote Multipart and arranged for the company to sponsor the SuperTruck Trophy Meeting at Silverstone. Peter was also the leading light behind the breathtaking *Skytrain* wheelie truck, piloted by Steve Murty, which appeared in 1986.

Previous page
Svempa Bergendahl, from Sweden, hand built his *Yellow Widow* from a Scania T112M. With the exception of the cab, all the bodywork, including the front air dam-cum-bumper, has been custom built from aluminium. Under the Scania's bonnet is no mean power unit; a DSC 11 litre engine modified to produce a staggering 900 bhp. This propels the truck from 0 to 60 mph in nine seconds flat, impressive even for a car. As you can imagine, the interior is just as modified, with a roll bar, Isringhausen racing seats, buttoned leather side panels and headlining, and a leather-trimmed steering wheel. Svempa spent 2000 hours building *Yellow Widow*. By the way, in Sweden, *Yellow Widow* is the nickname for a brand of champagne

Two race circuits had been approached with the idea of truck racing, but neither was completely sold on it. However, Donington, in the Midlands, did agree, so the venue was set for the first British event. At the time, no technical rules existed for the truck races held so far in Europe, so Chambers wrote a set of regulations, which are still the basic rules used today for the European Championship.

The Donington event, held in September 1984, attracted a crowd of over 80,000 people, who watched some 40 trucks put on a super day's racing. So many people turned up that the access roads were blocked, and the M1 motorway had a five-mile tail-back in each direction. This resulted in the county of Leicestershire gaining the record for the biggest ever traffic jam and achieving a place in the *Guinness Book of Records*.

As you will see from this book, that first event attracted many of Britain's leading drivers from several different motor sports. Many of them are still in there racing today, as are many professional truckers, who drive all week long, delivering all manner of goods throughout the UK and Europe.

Barry Sheene competed in that first British

Right
With a backdrop of pyramids, this MAN toughs it out in the Pharoahs Rally

Overleaf, left
An oil-splattered cab and smoke from a turbocharged engine are but part of the make-up of truck racing. Colin Redfern fires up his Detroit-powered Bedford TM after the Supergrid walk-about. With the ever-present threat of a turbo catching fire, it's a good idea to carry a fire extinguisher

Overleaf, right
America's version of the wheelie truck heads skywards. Appropriately, it is powered by a 2000 hp Allison V12 aircraft engine

race. The twice World Motorcycle
Champion drove a DAF 3300, the make he
continued to drive until his retirement in
1988, carrying the famous number 7 from his
bike-racing days. World Hot Rod Champions
Barry Lee and Paul Grimer also took part.
Lee drove a Ford Cargo in 1987 and worked
with Anglia Television at the Silverstone
SuperTruck meeting, his truck being
equipped with an on-board camera to put
viewers in the thick of the action. He was
also able to talk to the commentary team
during the race. World Stock Car Champion
Les Mitchell, Formula 1 driver Martin
Brundle and rally ace Andy Dawson drove
the Leyland tractor unit used by the
Williams Formula 1 team to transport their
racing cars.

Duilio Ghislotti, from Como, Italy, won the
1984 race in a Volvo F12 (the truck he used
for hauling loads to Britain), while Richard

Above
Age is not a barrier when it comes to drag
racing a truck. This old-timer must have
covered many thousands of miles in its time

Right
Lean and mean. This stripped and lowered
White belches plenty of smoke from its stacks
as it accelerates around the track

Walker, a haulier's son from
Nottinghamshire, who today is still one of
Britain's leading drivers, finished second.
Drivers from Holland, France, Sweden and
Germany also took part.

So truck racing was off and running in the
UK, and in 1985 a full European
Championship was held, with a total of
seven races, including the Multipart British
Grand Prix at Silverstone and the first Lucas

14

Truck Superprix at Brands Hatch. This circuit was treated with respect at the time, no one knowing what would happen if one of these seven tonne monsters crashed into the barriers, or if there was a multi-truck pile-up. Barry Lee volunteered to drive a truck into the 'arrestabed' trap at Druids hairpin, simulating brake failure, at 20, 40 and 60 mph. The gravel dragged the truck to a halt so rapidly that the rear wheels lifted. The drivers also tried Brands in the pre-1960s, anti-clockwise direction, but eventually they settled on the current, familiar clockwise direction.

The Italians, French, Swedes, Germans and Danes all participated in that first, successful European Championship, which was won by Rod Chapman in a Ford Cargo. His was a convincing win, being 15 points ahead of his nearest rival Richard Walker. Willie Green, the historic car racer, came third, scooping a hat-trick for the British drivers.

In 1986 the series was further expanded and again won by a British driver, Mel Lindsey, in a Leyland Roadtrain. Mel was one of the original professional truckers who turned up at Donington for the 1984 British race—his first time at a race circuit.

In 1987 there was even more racing, both in Britain and the rest of Europe, with a first event in Hungary, which had Russians,

Left
Beam axle, heavy anti-roll bar and large brake drums are all standard on Curt Goransson's Volvo N12. After two to three laps, particularly on a short, twisty circuit like Brands Hatch where the brakes must be used frequently, the brake drums and shoes become very hot and suffer from fade. At Zolder, however, the situation is even worse. Its high-speed straights and very tight corners lead to such heat build-up that tyres have been known to explode in the pits

Bulgarians and Czechs competing for the first time. A Hungarian racing truck and team also participated in the Lucas Truck Superprix at Brands Hatch that season. The Australians have adopted our brand of the sport, too, but ironically the Americans do not seem to have fared all that well over the past few years. Now their races are confined to dirt tracks after experiencing problems with the heavy trucks tearing up the paved circuits.

So what's involved in preparing a truck for racing? Firstly, any prospective racer must consider the class in which he or she wants to race. Running in the 361–450 hp class means spending plenty of money to be competitive. State of the art in this class, to my mind, are trucks such as Slim Borgudd's West Coast Diesel White Road Boss, and George Allen's White Road Boss. Perhaps it's the American look, as I have been hooked on US trucks for some years. There are plenty of good-looking fast trucks in this class, and last year I was lucky enough to get a ride in one of them, a Scammell S26 Cummins driven by Howard Barnes. You can read about that adventure elsewhere in this book.

The racing is close in the hotly-contested 300 hp class, too, and this type of racing might be a little kinder on the pocket.

Right

All makes and models of trucks are used for racing. The ideal is something that runs a big-capacity engine, or perhaps a turbo, in stock form, or a light truck with a turbocharged six- or eight-cylinder engine. Mike Booth chose a 1981 Bedford with a Detroit 6V92 V6 engine. A turbo plus supercharger helps to push in as much diesel as possible, but this can lead to problems with emitting too much black smoke—and that can lead to disqualification. Mike's mechanic is checking that the engine is revving to 2600 rpm and not pushing out too much smoke

Above
Line-up of Ford Cargo L10s. Left to right: Barry Lee, Rod Chapman, Divina Galica

Although a limited amount of modification is allowed, to qualify for racing, a truck must be in standard condition and to the manufacturer's specification. For safety reasons, the regulations insist on a roll cage, manufactured from approved materials, being fitted inside the cab. Most racers also install a pair of racing seats in place of the originals, and these are complemented by four-point harnesses that are essential for holding the driver (and any passenger) secure in the seat, particularly when cornering. A fire extinguisher is compulsory, and the driver must wear fireproof overalls, gloves and boots, together with a crash helmet.

Tyres of the lowest profile, but of the widest section available are fitted to the front, and part-worn tyres are allowed, provided they have a minimum tread depth of 5 mm. Depending on the circuit, tyres may last only 10–15 laps, so these are a major expense during a season's racing.

Overheating of brakes is a common problem when stock assemblies are used, and modified brake linings are permitted, together with cooling ducts. Even so, heat build-up can be excessive, leading, inevitably, to brake fade. At the time of writing, there is some controversy over a system used on some of the trucks, whereby the brakes are cooled by a water spray. One simple method of doing this is to spray

Above
Rod Chapman leads French entrant Noel
Crozier's Renault 290GT in the 300 hp race at
Silverstone. Noel, who runs his own 80-vehicle
haulage company, lives in Vorche, near St
Etiennne, in central France. He first raced in
Simca Rally 2, then moved on to Lola sports
cars. His first truck race was a Le Mans 24-hour
event in 1983. He finished third in that race,
driving a Renault

Overleaf
Among the Dutchmen at Brands Hatch in 1985
was Tony Pol, who drove this neat Ford all-out
racing truck

water on to the outside of the drum, but any
water not evaporated on contact with the hot
drum will be thrown out under the wing. A
more sophisticated method is to cool the
inside of the drum with a water spray. Both
methods are only used when necessary, and
there is always the possibility of cold water
hitting a hot drum and causing it to crack.

In the suspension department, the shock
absorbers, spring shackles and kingpins are
always of the best quality for stability
reasons. Rear axle ratios can be changed,
and usually the highest available are fitted.

Although engine modifications are
allowed, the basic engine has to be the same
as that fitted originally by the manufacturer.
If the truck began life with a 300 hp engine,
then that is what the racer has to work with.
It is quite possible to double the horsepower
by making changes to the turbocharging and
fuel pump, but the rules lay down that the

engine is governed to 2600 rpm at full throttle with no load. There are regulations limiting the amount of exhaust smoke a truck can emit, but too much smoke from the exhaust means an engine is not producing all of its potential horsepower.

Truck racing is a lot of fun, and whether you are standing on the sidelines watching, or drive a truck for a living and fancy taking part, you are sure to have a good time.

For their assistance in preparing this book, many thanks must go to: Brands Hatch Racing Circuit, Silverstone Racing Circuit, Peter Minnis of *Trucking International*, **Ben Mead** of *Truck & Driver*, **Andrew Frankl** of *TRUCK*, **Leyland DAF, MAN, photographers Bette S. Garber, Marty Hatfield, David Jacobs, Martin Sharp and Steve Sturgess,** and all the racers who took the time to fill in my questionaires.

Mike Key
February 1988

Left
Gaudenzio Mantova, from Italy, attempts a power-on 'doughnut' in the middle of the track at Silverstone. The truck is a Renault R390

Right
Birds' boss, that's Graham Levett, decided that at the end of 1986, Birds as a company would continue to be involved in truck racing, but would not use one of their fleet trucks. Instead, they would build a pure race truck for his son, Andrew, to drive. He set off for Holland with their mechanic, Andy Young, to look at a 1982 bonneted Scania, having been impressed with the Scania driven by Rolf Bjork. With half a million kilometers on the clock, it was clean and had been looked after, so they brought it back to their base in Warley, near Birmingham. The first job was to alter the 6 × 2 axle configuration to a 4 × 2 arrangement. A Fuller nine-speed gearbox was hooked up behind the V8 engine, which was stripped and carefully rebuilt with honed bores and polished bearings by Andy Young. His expertise netted approximately 1050 bhp. Birds' Scania sits on Aspect aluminium wheels shod with Pirelli low-profile tyres

Overleaf, left
Thomas Heggmann's Daimler-Benz 1638 sports a super, deep black paint job

Overleaf, right
Racing grandfather Alan Hodge, 52, is the pilot of this smart Perkins-powered ERF, run by his son, Chris. Theirs is one of the most professional teams in the sport. Alan raced in single-seater Formula 3 over 25 years ago

Thomas Hegmann
O +

in Faorila, Sweden, where he runs a timber haulage business operating five trucks, and presumably he developed his sideways driving technique while working in Sweden's wooded countryside, particularly during snowy winter weather. He made his truck-racing debut at Mantorp Park, Sweden, in 1985. After trying the sport and liking it, he decided to join the ETRO regulars in 1986 with an immaculate new Volvo and backing from Nynas, a Swedish oil company. In 1987 he appeared in another new Volvo N12 with sponsorship from Q8 oils. This had a sophisticated automatic transmission

Left

Swedes love a wide variety of motorsport, and they throw themselves wholeheartedly into whichever form they choose. All the drivers from Sweden rank high in truck racing. Rolf Bjork, the heavyweight haulier from Helsingborg, was the first to take to the tracks on a professional basis. He has competed in every British event since 1984. At that Donington Park event he raced his working truck, a Scania 140. This was equipped with a heavy sleeper cab, and he failed to make the final. Since then he has been racing his immaculate, bonneted Scania 142, with impressive results at British meetings. Careful preparation is the name of the game, although the trucks must be standard and meet the manufacturer's original specification. Rolf has devoted an enormous amount of time to training his mechanics, brothers Klaus and Tommy Anderson, who helped reinforce the chassis and build the skirted bodywork

Previous page, left
Johnny Harrera lights the tyres as he launches his 600 bhp Cummins-powered Freightliner down the quarter mile

Previous page, right
This bright-yellow, bonneted Renault CLM340 is piloted by Claude Cuynet from France. Claude raced in his first truck event in 1983 at Paul Ricard, where he also raced a Renault. Like many other racers, he has a history of racing cars, including—surprise, surprise—Renaults! Nice looking, these bonneted trucks. Wonder if the bumper-cum-air dam is stock?

Right
In the past, Curt Goransson, 1986 Multipart British Truck Grand Prix winner, was involved in rallying. He began his rallying career 20 years ago with a BMW, before moving on to a great deal of success with Opel. He also achieved a top-ten placing and was top privateer in one of the RAC rallies, driving an Audi Quattro. The 43-year-old Goransson lives

Above
Disappearing trucks from Copse Corner at Silverstone

Left
Mel Lindsey, 1986 European Truck Racing Champion and professional truck driver, checks his crash helmet before demonstrating the fun of truck racing to a journalist at Brands on press day

Right
Roy Clarke, of YT Truck Racing, looks pensive
as he waits on the grid for the start of the
301–360 hp race at Brands Hatch. Looks as
though his Detroit-powered Bedford TM has
suffered some bodily contact!

Above
Headlights blazing and trailing clouds of diesel smoke, Curt Goransson pushes his Volvo N12 hard

Right
Trucks waiting to be scrutinized after a race, to make sure they are legal and have been raced within the rules

Left
Aerodynamically-shaped bumper and roof panel, headlights crossed with tape in case of a mishap, and below the bumper two flared tubes to duct cooling air to the front brakes

Above
A Ford Cargo L10 entered by Anglia Television. The driver is Barry Lee, well known for his winning years in hot rod racing, where he powered his Escort to win at least 44 major championships. Barry competes in the hotly-contested 300 hp class, and the reason for the Anglia Television connection is because the truck had an on-board camera. Barry could also talk to the team of commentators to give the viewer a real in-depth look at the race. It worked well, too

Above

Michel Paquelet from Lyon, in France, powers his 1981 Iveco along the Cooper Straight at Brands Hatch. Gear changing on this truck is handled by a Fuller 12-speed gearbox. Most of the cab's interior has been stripped out to save weight, and a full regulation roll cage has been installed, together with a lightweight racing seat. Michel became interested in truck racing through an article in *France Routiers*, a French truck magazine

Right

Svempa Bergendahl demonstrates the acceleration of his slick Scania

The quiet of an early spring morning was broken by a crackling announcement over the pit tannoy, 'Drivers are ready. Crash helmets must be worn; they are available at each truck.' What's it like to ride around a race circuit in a race truck? I took the opportunity to answer this question at a press day at Brands Hatch. Scrambling up into the cab and manoeuvring one's body over the roll cage that seems to fill the cab and blocks half of the door opening is no mean feat in itself. The pit crew were on hand to advise on the full race harness as I settled into the racing seat, explaining that it had to be very tight as one could be thrown around in cornering manoeuvres. 'Okay,' I replied, 'but I need some room to move, at least to look to my right.' I wanted to take photos as we drove around, but I had not considered the difficulty of doing this while wearing a crash helmet. Equipped with my trusty Nikon, a small camera-mounted flash gun to light the interior of the cab, and the add-on motor drive, it was becoming difficult to actually see through the view finder, as I could not get the camera to my eye.

Howard Barnes, who is Scammell's marketing director, seemed interested in participating in my project. He holds the lap record at Silverstone in his 1982 Scammell S26. I had the impression, though, that it would be a doddle around the track—a couple of laps—as these trucks consume some seven gallons of fuel per race and three sets of brake pads in a weekend's racing. How wrong I was! Last words from the crew member who strapped me in were, 'Don't hold on to the roll cage across the door.' I wondered why.

Howard fired up the 14 litre Cummins engine and we trundled down the pit road towards the circuit. Receiving the all clear from the marshall, we shuddered out on to the track in eleventh gear, immediately rounding the sharp right-hander of Paddock and up into twelfth. At this time I was engaged in looking through the

camera and not where we were going, so I received a firm heave in the stomach as the truck lurched and swayed suddenly, dropping down to the bottom of Hailwood Hill. Beneath the Dunlop Bridge it was time to start braking for Druids, clipping the apex, and then it was down Graham Hill, entering Graham Hill Bend at 60 mph. The tyres protested with a fair amount of squealing, but once out of the bend and on to Cooper Straight, it was foot on the boards, driving on the governor (which limits the rpm to 2600). The left-hand Surtees followed by the right-hand McLaren needs a racing line that is as straight as possible. Next comes Clark Curve, and halfway round it's power on and tight into the final part of the bend, tyres protesting all the time. Then change up to thirteenth gear, cut across to the beginning of

the pit wall, flat out along Brabham Straight, topping around 90 mph, dropping down to twelfth for Paddock Hill Bend, and around we went again.

After the first few laps, I began to appreciate the thrill of it all. Hanging in the harness was like being a puppet on strings, being thrown around. With such a high centre of gravity, the cab moved around a lot, and the door moved in and out in relation to the roll cage, hence the crew member's last words. I could also see why there was a need for a full harness. Howard kept that truck rolling round for many laps, no pussy footing. He did, in fact, lap Brands in around 1 minute, 5 seconds—as fast as when he races. Here, we are following the racing line of the truck in front out of Clark Curve. I would not have missed it for anything!

Above left

Gertie, the Lucas CAV team's first truck, is believed to be the first European truck specifically built for racing. It was prepared by Leyland France in 1983, and driven to third place in that year's Le Mans 24-hour truck race by Dave Gray and Mel Bacon. Subsequently, the left-hand-drive 360 hp Leyland Roadtrain had a long and successful career with Mel Bacon as driver. Over the winter of 1986–87, *Gertie Mk 2*

was built, now with right-hand-drive. During the following season, the truck was driven by Stan Hart, with Peter Duncan from the TV series *Duncan Dares* as co-driver

Above

George Allen guns his 9 litre Detroit Diesel powered White Road Boss, sponsored by his company Truck Align

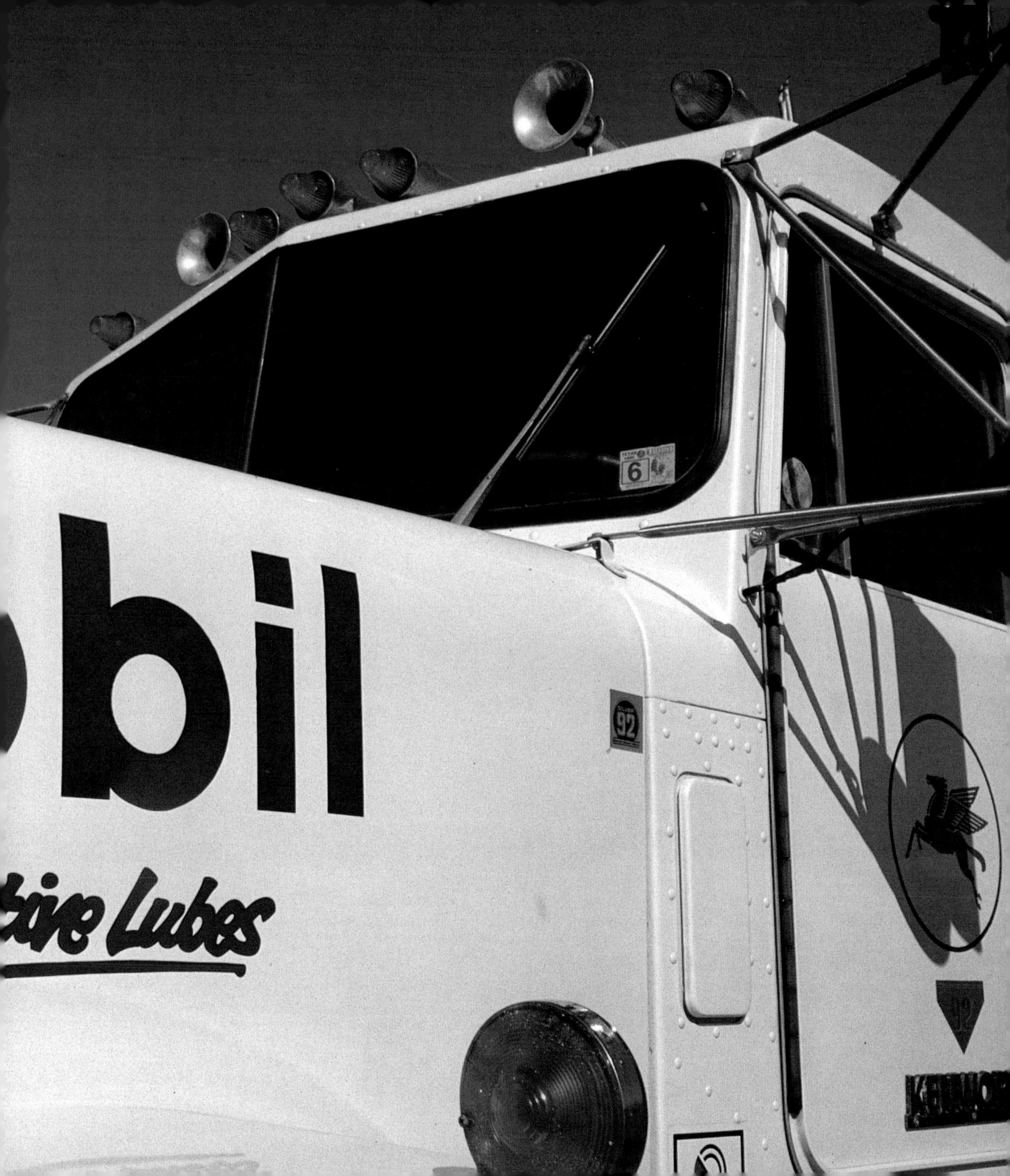
bil
Lubes

Previous page, left
Good rear-view mirrors are essential
equipment for observing those approaching
from behind. The external air cleaner
completes that American look

Previous page, right
Front shot is all American

Above
Dusk falls at the dragstrip and another Mack
roars down the quarter mile

Right
Kenworth 'cab-over' at speed on the strip

44

Steve Murty had this idea, 'How about putting a jet airplane engine into a Ford Cargo?' In 1982 he approached Ford and Pirelli with the idea, and the result was the *Pirelli Pro-Jet*. The *Pro-Jet* is based on a standard Ford Cargo 0918, but the original engine and transmission have been replaced by a Rolls-Royce Avon gas turbine, developing 12,200 lb of thrust (enough to push the truck to an 11.84 second quarter-mile time with a terminal speed of 135 mph, making it the fastest truck in Europe). The truck's chassis was widened to accept the turbine engine, which is mounted low on stainless-steel hoops. The original front axle and steering assembly have been retained, and the cab is in the usual position, allowing air for the engine to be drawn through the normal grille and under the floor. Safety for the driver is of the utmost importance, as with all racing trucks, so a six-point roll cage was constructed from 2 in. diameter, $\frac{1}{4}$ in. thick seamless steel tubing. An aircraft-style Simpson five-point harness keeps the driver in his seat, and aircraft gauges fill the original Cargo dash. In place of the original rev counter is a turbine-speed gauge, the speedometer has been replaced by an airspeed indicator calibrated in hundreds of knots, and the engine's throttle lever is where the gear lever used to be. Next to the throttle is the release for the twin 2 m diameter parachutes, which assist in braking the truck at speeds between 70 mph and 150 mph. Below 70 mph the truck's normal brakes are used. These are air/hydraulic units taken from a 15 tonne Cargo. Custom-built fuel tanks at each side of the chassis hold 300 litres each to cope with the engine's full-throttle consumption of 4.5 litres per second. The alloy tanks have recesses to accommodate the battery to power the instruments on one side, and the brake reservoir tanks on the other. The *Pro-Jet*'s dazzling custom paintwork is a combination of Fireball red over Aztec gold on a white Pearl base. The 19 coats of paint have been finished

with six coats of clear lacquer. To add to the sparkle, the truck is fitted with a set of polished Alcoa forged-aluminium wheels shod, of course, with Pirelli Hi-speed truck tyres. These have been buffed down to 3 mm tread depth to reduce centrifugal mass

Above
Divina Galica is one of three women involved in truck racing. Here, the former Olympic ski-captain chases Gaudenzio Mantova into the chicane at Silverstone. Divina drives one of the Ford Cargos in the Rod Chapman/Mike Smith team

Right
ERF B driven by Tony Chesney at Silverstone

Above
Three European countries are represented in this picture: 25, Gerard Cuynet, from France, Ford Cargo; 31 (centre), Reima Soderman, from Finland, Sisu SR; Mel Lindsey, Great Britain, Leyland Roadtrain

Right
French driver Pascal Robineau battles through clouds of diesel smoke in his Volvo F10 at Silverstone

50

Above
Polished Alcoa wheels shod with Pirelli tyres keep this MAN 560 hp truck on the circuit at Brands Hatch. A turbo helps to keep the power coming, and gear-changing is handled by a 16 ZF Ecosplit

Right
A Guy Big J4T, with a Perkins engine and running in the 300 hp class, is an unusual sight on the race track. It must have been around for some 15 years, being owned by Jeff Mason and driven by Mel Bacon. It is very competitive too, having won several races

Above

Exhaust stacks were popular when truck racing began back in 1984. In 1987, however, in an effort to improve performance, many racers have gone to side pipes. The only problem with these is the build-up of diesel smoke behind the front runners, which makes life difficult for the photographer who wants to snap the rest of the field!

Above
Flag waving during the grand parade is the in
thing, whether it is for your country or sponsor

Left
The V8 diesel engine in Graham Levett's Scania

Right
Neat, turbocharged Cummins inline diesel engine in Gary Hodkinson's 1977 ERF. Note that air and diesel enter the engine on the left, and exhaust gases leave on the right through the turbo and a short exhaust pipe—no stacks

Previous page, main pic
Two wheels or six? Steve Parrish, former British Motorcycle Champion, seems to be equally at home riding a four-cylinder 750 cc Yamaha, with an output of 120 bhp in racing trim, and the Mitchell Cotts Mercedes 1644, with its 14.62 litre V8, twin-turbo intercooled engine that puts out 440 bhp as standard. What is the difference between throwing a two-wheeled bike around Brands Hatch and lapping the circuit in a six-wheeled truck? 'It's a fair bit quicker on a bike. Last year my best lap on the Yamaha was around 49 seconds (average speed 88 mph); the truck lap record stands at one minute, four seconds (average speed 67.49 mph). It's in the stopping, when you realize that a seven tonne truck at 100 mph takes a lot more stopping than 400 lb of motorcycle at 150! As the Mercedes has a tremendous amount of torque, I only need to use two gears, that's fifteenth and sixteenth. On the Yamaha we have to use all six on every lap at Brands Hatch.'

Previous page, inset
Tony Jenkins in a full sideways slide in his Scammell S26 at Brands Hatch

Above
Mel Lindsey has a reputation for being a hard driver and occasionally minor scrapes occur. Here, the team, including Mel, sets to work on the newly-painted Leyland Roadtrain's bumper

Left
Mike Smith, well known radio and TV personality, made his truck-racing debut at Brands in 1986, when he shocked the establishment by taking overall victory in the up to 300 hp class races. 'Smithy's' extensive saloon-car racing experience came in handy as he powered his Ford Cargo to victory by fractions of a second over the truck's owner, Rod Chapman. Although Stormont sponsors Rod Chapman, Divina Galica and Mike Smith, when all three are on the track there are no team rules regarding who will take the lead. This produces some really close door-handle to door-handle racing

Above
The Hodge team manhandle a new gearbox into
their ERF. They worked furiously in the pits to
change the box—it's all heavyweight stuff!

Overleaf
Steve Murty achieved a world record by
piloting his *Skytrain* wheelie truck for an official
distance of 319.8 m at Silverstone. The truck is
based on a Leyland Landtrain 19.24, which is
built to operate in the most adverse conditions
of third-world countries. This means it is strong
enough to withstand the impact of crash landings
from 10 ft wheelies at 40 mph. The chassis has
been shortened to give a wheelbase of 3.79 m,
and a sliding ballast box has been added
beneath the aircraft-style wing. This is movable
by means of hydraulic rams, so the vehicle can
be made road legal and driven to events. On
arrival, the ballast can be adjusted to allow for
track conditions and headwind etc, helping to
keep the truck balanced when the front wheels
come off the ground. Power to pull giant
wheelies comes from a Cummins NTE350
big-cam diesel engine, which is turbocharged
and fitted with an air-to-water intercooler. The
14 litre engine has been modified to produce
around 500 bhp, with 1400 lb ft of torque at the
flywheel. A ZF Ecomat five-speed fully
automatic gearbox with torque converter
multiplies that torque figure to a massive
.17,248 lb ft which, in turn, means that the pinion
climbs around the crown wheel with a force of
approximately 20 tons—sufficient to lift the front
of the 15 ton truck 15 ft in the air. Gear
changing is controlled by a micro processor,
which has been specially programmed for the
needs of the wheelie truck. The micro
processor also contains a second programme
for road driving, and this is available by simply
flicking a switch in the cab. A Leyland
heavy-duty 11 ton hub reduction axle
completes the drive train

Part of Motoring
DANA
GOODING GROUP LTD
GOODING GROUP LTD
Diesel Recon UK
Cummins
ReCon
Transmissio
BP
PIRELLI
The Wheelie Truck
Oils
Shell

Above
Hugger Orange paint makes this Seddon
Atkinson 401 really stand out on the
truck-racing circuits. It is driven by Steve
Howson, who has only been racing for two
seasons. *Second Attempt* is powered by a
300 hp Gardner engine backed up by a Fuller
9513 gearbox. Steve reckons he can lap Brands
Hatch in his Pirelli-shod truck in 1 minute,
9 seconds

Right
The Red Light Racing team's Dodge with
Adrian Kidd behind the wheel at Silverstone

Shell Oils
MULTIPART
SUPERTRUCK TROPHY '87
MULTIPART
Turbo
MULTIPART
70
Perkins
Perkins
Shell Oils
Fuels and Lubricants
Shell Oils
Fuels and Lubricants

Above
Ready to launch. A drag-racing Peterbilt 'conventional' on the start line with full staging lanes behind

Right
With exhaust stacks trailing twin plumes of diesel smoke, this International sets off on a trip down the quarter mile

Above

Obviously, in racing, there is the ever-present danger of accidents, and truck racing is no different. In fact, when you look at the physical size of the trucks, it is a wonder that there is not more vehicle contact. On the first lap of the hotly-contested 301–360 hp race at Silverstone, there was a little bumping and jiving, to say the least, resulting in the race being stopped to clear the track. Tony Pond's Leyland Roadtrain can be seen being towed away by one of the heavy wreckers in attendance

Right

Unfortunately, Henry Shepherd's ERF lost a door skin in the incident at Silverstone. The race was restarted after the assembled drivers were given a knuckle-rapping by the race director, Pierre Aumonier

Above
These French guys must have more practice at
this game than the Brits. Robineau Pascal won
the Le Mans 24-hour race in 1975. He drives a
1975 Volvo F10 with a turbocharged TD101F
engine. The gearbox is a Volvo SR62, tyres are
22.5 in. by 315.80 Firestones, and the paint,
need I say, is brilliant yellow

Right
Wheel-to-wheel racing is common on the
American oval tracks. Here, the pack is led
down the straight by a neat, open-wheel White

Overleaf, left
Leyland's Cabriolet, used as a pace truck,
keeps the pack together on the warm-up lap

Overleaf, right
A talented trucker without doubt, 33-year-old
Richard Walker, manager of the Toxford-based
family haulage concern, came into truck racing
after previous success in various forms of
off-road motorsport, in particular grasstrack
racing and special stage rallying. Richard's
1983 Leyland Roadtrain is equipped with a
Cummins engine and Fuller gearbox

Shell Oils
MULTIPART
SUPERTRUCK TROPHY '87
MULTIPART
LEYLAND
340 CHARGECOOLED
C152 KRN
TRUCK&DRIVER magazine
TRUCK&DRIVER magazine

Above
Looks like Barry Lee is giving Mel Lindsey a hard time coming out of Copse Corner at Silverstone

Right
Spinner of the year was how accident-prone Reg Hopkins described himself—he has spun on every track in Europe. Reg was into stock cars, then horse racing, until he was 38. Then he got into truck racing. Wonder which taught him his spinning trick? His 1981 Leyland Roadtrain is powered by a 14 litre Cummins 290E, with turbo and modified fuel-injection system. All this power is backed up by a Fuller 9509A nine-speed gearbox. The other two members of his team, Philip and Oliver, helped Reg build the truck from two write-offs. Reg is affectionately known as 'Reg the Sledge' after he buried a sledgehammer in the radiator of his truck while trying to straighten a bent bumper!

Left

Barry Sheene, twice World Motorcycle
Champion, needs no introduction. Barry really
enjoyed his truck racing; he had been involved
right from the beginning of the sport in Britain
and raced a DAF in the 301–360 hp class, until
he retired in 1988. He used to drive a truck for
a living before he became a motorcycle star

Above

It's a long way up from a kart to a racing truck,
but Gerd Korber has made the transition and he
is doing fine in the 360 hp class, picking up
regular rostrum placings in Austria and
Germany. Korber drives the Bickel-Tuning
MAN 19,332

Left
A name that was prominent in truck racing
during 1987 is Truck Align, who not only
sponsored their own racers, but also helped
other racers in trouble, among them Barry
Sheene, who wrecked his DAF on the Friday
before the start of the season at Brands. Truck
Align rebuilt Barry's truck overnight. George
Allen owns and runs the company with the help
of his brother Les. Both race trucks. George is
one of the few drivers who had no previous
experience of circuit racing before he started
truck racing. He became interested in the sport
in 1985 when they repaired an Italian-owned
DAF that had been damaged at Silverstone. In
1986 he became 'Rookie of the Year', driving a
bright-yellow White Commander, powered by
a Caterpillar engine, in the 360 hp class. For
1987 George decided to build himself a new
truck based on a bonneted White Road Boss,
similar to the one driven by Slim Borgudd in
1986. With the help of Murray Kerohan, who has
been working full-time on the project, he
assembled the truck from the chassis rails up.

Power comes from a 9 litre Detroit Diesel,
which George rebuilt with a supercharger and
turbocharger, and it is expected to produce 600
horsepower

Above
Dick Pountain, whose ERF B-series is sponsored
by his own company, Pountains Heavy Haulage,
is typical of the many truck drivers who enjoy a
weekend's fun driving their own truck on the
racing circuit, and are back using it in the
haulage business during the week

Overleaf, left
Steve Horne smoking his ERF B-series along the
Brabham Straight at Brands Hatch

Overleaf, right
Truck Align sponsor several truck racers,
among them Les Allen. His Bedford TM has a
Detroit V6 engine backed up by a Fuller
nine-speed gearbox. This truck laps Brands
Hatch in 1 minute 7 seconds

Above
The pit crew hard at work on the Mitchell Cotts Mercedes V8 at Silverstone. The twin turbos (one for each bank of cylinders) at the rear of the engine are having their diesel/air-intake pipes checked before a day's racing

Left
Flip-front bonnet gives good access to the engine of George Allen's White Road Boss

Overleaf, inset
Among those racers still using exhaust stacks is Finn Jensen, from Denmark, who has a pair on his Iveco 190.42, and he is proud to demonstrate them while warming up the race truck in the pits

Overleaf, main pic
Squeezing as much horsepower as possible out of a turbo diesel engine can sometimes cause overheating and a breakdown of the turbo itself. This causes air and diesel to be pumped into the hot exhaust system, hence plenty of smoke. It's a good job the Jaguar fire tender is always close at hand

Previous page, main pic
Lots of diesel smoke after rounding Copse
Corner at Silverstone. The truck on the right
makes for the edge of the track with a possible
turbo fire

Previous page, inset
A short exhaust pipe blows diesel smoke out of
the back of Tony Jenkins' Scammell S26 as he
leans right going through the chicane at
Woodcote Corner, Silverstone. A stock turbo
set-up pumps air and diesel into the 14 litre
Cummins engine, which is backed up by a
Fuller nine-speed gearbox

Above
Supergrid walk-about at Brands Hatch not only
gives the photographer an opportunity for
some long telephoto shots, but also allows the
public the opportunity to meet and talk to the
drivers

Above
Race order has to be adhered to. Here, a race marshall checks out Brian Garnett in his Leyland Buffalo before he is allowed on to the circuit at Brands. This truck is powered by a Leyland TL11 engine, the only Leyland engine racing

Right
One of the better turned out trucks in Britain is Alan Hodge's ERF

Above
Gertie Mk 2 undergoing extensive repairs to
the turbo in the pits at Silverstone

Above
Belching diesel smoke, Jean-Pierre Stalder's
Volvo makes an unusual sight on the race track

Above
Slim Borgudd's turbocharged V8 engine,
prepared by West Coast Diesel

Right
One of the team's mechanics works on the
turbocharged Gardner engine in Steve
Howson's Seddon Atkinson 401. The clean
engine is set off with a splash of chrome on the
rocker cover

Left
Tym Oostenbrugge has been racing his trusty 1973 Scania Vabis 110 Super for six years, and it is still running strong. Its 295 hp diesel engine was fitted with a turbocharger as original equipment, and it is backed by a ten-speed gearbox

Above
Swiss driver Jean-Pierre Stalder hauls his Volvo around the racing line, just ahead of British driver Adrian Kidd in his Dodge K300

Above
In 1985, at Brands Hatch, Aad Van Koeveringe headed a six-truck Dutch contingent in the unlimited Thunder Truck races. Aad raced this super looking American Peterbilt, which he had recently imported from the USA at a price of £55,000. It ran fast on the straights, but used most of the track to negotiate the corners at Brands

Above
A shot from the good old days. A Peterbilt
'conventional' looks the business on a tarmac
oval track in the USA

Above
Kenworth and Mack drag it out after darkness

Right
In truck pulls, trucks compete against each other, pulling special weighted sleds. As they strain to move the heavy weights, they often lift their front wheels off the ground. Here, Ernie Nietzger's Kenworth, *The Liberty Belle*, goes like the clappers

Centre right
Ernie Nietzger also owns this Kenworth, *The General Lee*

Bottom right
Shirley Garrard's GMC lifts its front wheels well clear of the ground in a truck pull

Overleaf, left
After dark on the dragstrip, the roaring trucks seem even more monstrous. Even oldies can come out to play

Overleaf, right
Here, a Freightliner squares off against a Mack. Note the timing-light beams hitting the front tyre

Above
Anything seems to go in American truck drag racing—including racing heavy-duty wreckers!

Right
On the grand parade, Gerrit Hultink, from the Netherlands, proudly proclaimed that his Scania 110 Super is 26 years old and still racing!

Above

The other half of the Lucas CAV team is *Flo*, driven by Dave Gray. *Flo* is powered by a factory-prepared Perkins Eagle 290L motor and runs in the 300 hp class. This gives the team shots at two power categories. *Flo*'s co-driver is mother of two, Pauline Stewart, who holds an HGV licence, as do all the drivers in truck racing. Pauline became interested in racing while working for PA Haulage, a transport company run by Phil Morris

Above
One of the most decorative trucks to come out
of Italy is Giovanni Bellichi's Iveco 190, which
has extensive murals. It takes hundreds of
hours to achieve a finish like this. Hopefully, he
won't put it into the Armco

Above

Barry Sheene, still sporting the number 7 from
his motorcycle racing days, speeds past the
grandstand at Brands. The truck had been
rebuilt the night before by Truck Align after a
bad spin, during a practice session, caused
considerable damage to the chassis and cab of
the Sherwood Trucks DAF

Right

Mike Booth leads Gary Hodkinson in the grand
parade of racing trucks at Silverstone. With that
size of hand, it's a good job the drivers are not
under the hand-signal rules!

Left
Gerd Korber, a former kart racer from
Germany, drives Bickel Tuning's MAN 19.332 in
the 360 hp class. He was the surprise of 1987,
picking up rostrum places in Austria and
Germany, and regularly gathering points to
hold third in this fiercely-contested class

Above
There does not seem to be many of these
bonneted Iveco trucks in the racing game.
However, Dante Mandrelli, from Italy, uses his
super red 190 PAC 26, which develops some
260 horsepower with the aid of a turbo
intercooler. The truck has an eight-speed
gearbox, and is unusual because of its
externally-mounted roll cage

Above

Not surprisingly, Heinz Dehnhardt, from Germany, races one of the big Mercedes Benz 1644 trucks. The 56-year-old runs his own transport business and sponsors his own truck. Heinz caught the truck-racing bug from his first race at Le Mans, in 1983. Until then, his only experience of racing was on two wheels, in motocross, in which he competed professionally until he was 29. Nowadays, his motorcycling is confined to the road, where he rides a 1000 cc BMW. The Mercedes is equipped with a big 14.62 litre, twin-turbo V8 engine, putting it into the 360 hp+ category. The massive engine is rumoured to pump out well over 1000 bhp

Above

When asked how he got involved with truck racing, the 1986 European Truck Racing Champion, Mel Lindsey, replied, 'It was a joke—with a brand-new, three-axle F12'. That was in 1984 and the first ever truck race in Great Britain at Donington Park, where Mel finished as a tail-ender. He progressed to scoring points regularly in 1985 with an F10 Volvo retired from the Rayleigh Cold Stores fleet, and in 1986 competed in ETRO, driving a Perkins-powered Leyland Roadtrain. With this, he accumulated the highest number of points to take the Championship. Mel is a professional trucker of 16 years standing; he spends five to six days a week pounding up and down motorways delivering meat. In 1987 he raced a 1985 Leyland Roadtrain equipped with a turbocharged, 12 litre Perkins straight-six and Fuller nine-speed gearbox

Left

Brake fade, caused by the heat generated between shoe and drum during racing, has been a problem since the first attempts at throwing these giants of the road around tight racing circuits, primarily designed for lighter racing and sports cars. In an effort to overcome the problem, larger shoes (seen in the foreground) are fitted to the standard drums, and some manufacturers are producing non-asbestos brake shoes for trucks. In one race, Tony Jenkins in his Scammell S26 Cummins went well past the brake fade point when the brakes caught fire. He dived into the pits at Brands where the crew extinguished the blaze and removed a very hot brake drum

Above
Two French drivers battle it out at Silverstone's Copse Corner. Noel Crozier drives the black Renault, and Gerard Cuynet the Ford DWAK BW

Right
Gerd Korber's mechanic checks out the fluids in the MAN engine before racing

Above

Swedish drivers tend to favour the long-bonneted Scanias and Volvos. Thordan Sjogren, from Bandhagen in Sweden, says he can power his Volvo N10, with its TD100 engine backed up by an R16 gearbox, around Brands Hatch in 1 minute, 5.9 seconds. Thordan explains his involvement in racing by saying that he is simply an 'old trucker', although now he is an ambulance driver

Right

Slim Borgudd has one of the best turned out trucks on the ETRO circuit, an American White Road Boss. The fabulous looking truck has clean white paint with Pearl flip-flop that bursts into a rainbow of colours in the light of the sun. It made its debut in April 1986, but its performance at that first meeting did not match the appearance. West Coast Diesel traced the fault to the microchip circuit in the Allison automatic gearbox, and with the problem cured the White turned into a real flyer, finishing 1986 by winning the 360 hp Championship and taking third overall in the outright European Championship. Slim now lives in Stratford-upon-Avon, and he began his racing career back in 1971 when he took up racing cars at club level. Since that time, he has driven in Formula Ford, Sports Car, Formula 3 and even Formula 1, so he is no stranger to the racing circuits. His introduction to truck racing came in August 1985 at Silverstone, where he drove Stan Williamson's Bedford to third place in the 300 hp class. In 1987 he was out in front at both Brands and Silverstone. Slim's driving is smooth and generally rhythmic—not surprising when you consider that he used to be the drummer in the backing group for the Swedish band ABBA

Above
Approaching Copse Corner at Silverstone: 1,
Richard Walker, Century Oils, Leyland
Roadtrain; 28, Gerd Korber, from Germany,
Bickel-Tuning Gmbh, Top-Sleeper + Trucker
Zubehor, MAN 19,332; 7, Barry Sheene,
Sherwood DAF Trucks, DAF F3600 DKX; 51,
Stan Hart, Lucas CAV, Leyland T45 Roadtrain,
Gertie

Above
George Allen in the White Road Boss 11 is hot
on the heels of Willie Green in the ERF
E14-35ST. Willie and Silkolene began their
partnership at Donington in 1984 at the first
British truck race. The ERF is powered by a
14 litre Cummins NTE 350 six-cylinder, inline
engine, which is turbocharged and aftercooled.
The gearbox is a Fuller Twin-Splitter

Above
Rod Chapman was a latecomer to truck racing; his first event was the Lucas Superprix at Brands Hatch in 1985, whereas most other regular drivers seem to have been into the sport right from the start, in 1984. However, Rod's white Ford Cargo was impressive right from its debut. The lightweight Cargo has always been fast and nimble around the tight circuit at Brands. Rod Chapman is based in Tunbridge Wells, and he drives in the 300 hp class. He is no stranger to racing, either, being an experienced rallycross driver

Right
Many of the truck racers have a history in racing of some form, and Les Mitchell is no exception—he has been British Stock Car Champion four times. Les chose a 1979–80 Spanish Dodge, which is helped along by a turbo and a Fuller manual gearbox. He pushes the seven-year-old Dodge around Brands in 1 minute 11 seconds

Above
Trucks take moving billboards to the extreme—
MAN support truck on the Paris–Dakar Rally

Right
The Paris–Dakar Rally attracts entries from all
over the world—even from behind the 'Iron
Curtain', as this Tatra demonstrates

Above
Battling up the beach is this MAN, a support vehicle in the Paris–Dakar Rally

Right
Dancing in the dunes. A MAN kicks up some sand as it tackles the Paris–Dakar

Overleaf
A rugged DAF 3600 tackles some typically-tough terrain in the gruelling Paris–Dakar Rally

Above
Even tough trucks need beefing up to survive the Paris–Dakar Rally. Note the roll cage and bull bars on this Mercedes

Right
The Paris–Dakar Rally is renowned as a killer of men and machines. This truck is one of the less serious casualties

Overleaf
When the going gets tough . . . A MAN travels at speed through the desert on its way to Dakar